The Crypto Arms Race

Evaluating the Security of Blockchain Applications

Table of Contents

Chapter 1. Introduction

In this Special Report, we introduce you to "The Crypto Arms Race: Evaluating the Security of Blockchain Applications"-- a comprehensive exploration of the rapidly evolving world of cryptocurrencies and the challenges that come with securing blockchain applications. However daunting this technical terrain may seem, we've meticulously demystified it for you, detailing everything from the patterns of advancement in crypto tech, to the security barriers and how they're being overcome. Why? Because we believe that everyone, regardless of their tech-savviness, should be able to participate in this ground-breaking era of digital transformation. All it takes is a bit of understanding, and that's precisely what this report aims to offer. So, whether you're looking to invest in crypto or simply want to expand your knowledge, this Special Report is undoubtedly an invaluable guide that could spark your crypto journey. Jump in, and let's navigate this fascinating realm together.

Chapter 2. The Rise of Cryptocurrencies: A Background

It all began in 2009, with the invention of Bitcoin by the anonymous entity known as Satoshi Nakamoto. Despite initial skepticism, Bitcoin's novel use of blockchain technology — a decentralized ledger that records transactions across multiple computers — paved the way for a new digital frontier.

2.1. The Idea Behind Bitcoin

With Bitcoin, Satoshi Nakamoto set out to solve one of digital cash's most pressing problems: double-spending. Prior to Bitcoin, digital currencies failed because there lacked a way to prevent one entity from spending the same amount twice. Bitcoin solved this double-spending problem without the need for a reliable intermediary. The decentralized nature of Bitcoin — it relies on consensus among its users — erases the need for central authorities and makes it an entirely peer-to-peer electronic cash system.

2.2. The Technology Behind Bitcoin

Bitcoin's core technology is the blockchain, a public, unchangeable ledger. It records every transaction ever made, in 'blocks', which are then linked together in a 'chain'. This decentralization means that no single entity can control the record of transactions. Further assurance of Bitcoin's security comes from the process known as 'mining.' This process involves complex cryptographic puzzles that the 'miners' solve to add the next block to the chain. The nature of these problems means they cannot be solved by brute force but instead require significant computational power.

2.3. Emergence of Altcoins

Following the success of Bitcoin, a host of other cryptocurrencies, known as altcoins (alternative coins), began to blossom. Each proposes unique characteristics that distinguish it from Bitcoin. For example, Ethereum introduced "smart contracts," self-executing contracts with the terms of the agreement directly written into lines of code. Meanwhile, Ripple focused on optimizing the financial sector's operational efficiency, serving as both a digital payment protocol and a cryptocurrency.

2.4. The Role of ICOs

Another milestone in the evolution of cryptocurrencies was the introduction of Initial Coin Offerings (ICOs). This crowdfunding method enables startups to raise capital by selling their own tokens to investors. Apart from investment, these tokens often serve other purposes within their native ecosystems, making cryptocurrencies not only a medium of exchange but also a facilitator of technological innovation.

2.5. The Dark Side of Cryptocurrencies

However, the increased popularity of cryptocurrencies brought challenges. The anonymous nature of cryptocurrency transactions has led it to become a favored means of transaction for illicit activities. Additionally, exchange platforms have become prime targets for hacker attacks, leading to enormous financial losses.

2.6. Decentralized Finance (DeFi)

More recently, Decentralized Finance (or DeFi) emerged as a new concept in the crypto space. It aims to create a financial system that is open to everyone and doesn't require intermediaries like banks. DeFi platforms allow users to lend or borrow funds from others, speculate on price movements on a range of assets using derivatives, trade cryptocurrencies, insure against risks, and earn interest in savings-like accounts.

2.7. The Future of Cryptocurrencies

The rise of cryptocurrencies shines a spotlight on a currency future where decentralization, privacy, and global access stand at its core. Yet, the path is fraught with numerous technological and regulatory challenges. Combined with volatility issues and potential for misuse, this future holds incredible promise and considerable risks. However, the current trends show growing acceptance of cryptocurrency across businesses and regulatory bodies alike.

Cryptocurrencies have come a long way since Bitcoin's initiation. The advent of altcoins and DeFi, and ICOs' proliferation points to an evolving crypto landscape with immense potential. A careful balance between regulation and innovation could solidify cryptocurrencies' position as a future-forward solution in the global financial landscape.

Through education and proper regulatory frameworks, stakeholders can unlock this potential while mitigating the associated risks. As we move forward in this exciting era of digital currencies, one thing seems certain: the rise of cryptocurrencies marks just the beginning of a teeming future crafted at the nexus of technology and finance.

In subsequent chapters, we'll delve further into the nuts and bolts of blockchain technology, highlighting its promise, its perils, and its potential to reshape our world.

Chapter 3. A Primer on Blockchain Technology

Understanding blockchain technology begins with acknowledging its most successful and popular application to date: Bitcoin. Proposed in a 2008 white paper by the pseudonymous 'Satoshi Nakamoto', Bitcoin offers an electronic payment system based on cryptographic proof instead of trust, permitting two willing parties to transact with each other without the necessity of a trusted third party.

3.1. The Genesis of Blockchain

In the context of cryptocurrencies like Bitcoin, blockchain technology serves as a public ledger for all transaction data from the start. When Satoshi Nakamoto introduced Bitcoin, he either inadvertently or deliberately also introduced blockchain to the world. A simple analogy to understand blockchain would be to imagine a growing chain of blocks. Each block, packed to the brim with transaction information, is unalterable and becomes a part of the immutable chain upon validation.

A transparent, peer-reviewed, and decentralized system, blockchain technology makes the alteration or deletion of information virtually impossible. It employs complex cryptographic principles and a consensus mechanism to maintain its immutability.

3.2. Elements of the Blockchain

To better understand this complicated technology, let's dissect the basic elements of a blockchain:

- **Block**: Each block on the network carries a list of transactions. Each new block contains a reference (hash) to the previous block and a timestamp, making it part of a continuous chain of blocks.

- **Transactions**: A transaction signifies any action that modifies the stored data. In the case of cryptocurrencies, it represents a transfer of value.

- **Hash**: The cryptographic hash function plays an essential role in maintaining the integrity of the block and the chain. Any slightest modification within the block alters the hash drastically, immediately flagging the tampering.

- **Nodes**: Nodes are user-run network mechanisms that validate and relay transactions, adding an extra layer of security.

3.3. Blockchain Types

Blockchains can be broadly placed in one of the following three categories:

1. **Public blockchains:** These are permissionless and open to anyone who wishes to participate. They offer incentives for their participants and are decentralized. Bitcoin and Ethereum are such examples.

2. **Private blockchains:** These only allow participation through invitations and are permissioned. They are mainly used for business purposes - for example, Hyperledger Fabric.

3. **Consortium blockchains:** Also known as federated blockchains, they are controlled by a group rather than a single entity and are semi-decentralized.

3.4. The Advent of Smart Contracts

With Ethereum's advent, blockchain stretched its wings beyond cryptocurrency and introduced the concept of "Smart Contracts" - a game-changer for blockchain applicability in various sectors. These self-executing contracts carry the terms of agreement directly written into code. When certain pre-set conditions get fulfilled, the smart contracts execute themselves.

3.5. Decentralized Applications (DApps)

Furthering the smart contract utility, developers began creating decentralized applications (DApps). Think of these as a regular online application, but instead of a traditional backend, they have smart contracts. By eliminating the central authority, these apps offer exponential advantages over regular apps, including censorship resistance, improved privacy, reduced downtime, and they often come with native monetization strategies.

3.6. Consensus Mechanisms

For a blockchain to work effectively, it needs to achieve consensus, namely, the participants need to agree on a single version of the truth. There are majorly two consensus mechanisms - Proof of Work (PoW), employed by Bitcoin, and Proof of Stake (PoS), adopted by Ethereum 2.0. Both possess their unique set of benefits and limitations. While PoW is highly secure, it is resource-intensive. PoS, on the other hand, provides energy efficiency but has its security concerns.

3.7. The Paradox of Blockchain

While blockchain's decentralization and transparency promise disruptive potential, they also entail some of the technology's key challenges, including performance and scalability issues, privacy dilemmas, and regulatory concerns.

Blockchain technology, a complex mix of cryptography, data structures, consensus algorithms, and incentive engineering, holds the promise of groundbreaking applications beyond the sphere of digital currency. As with any transformative technology, only time and experimentation will reveal the spectrum of its potential.

This ever-evolving world of blockchain technology, while teeming with opportunities, is not without risks. That's where understanding the inherent security features and possible vulnerabilities of blockchain applications becomes critical, and that's where we turn our attention next. But, that's another chapter in this expansive tale.

Chapter 4. Understanding Cryptographic Security

A crucial element in comprehending the security of blockchain is understanding cryptographic security. This involves recognising the intricacies of how cryptography functions and how it is utilised within the blockchain to maintain security and secrecy.

4.1. What is Cryptography?

Cryptography is a method that allows the secure transfer of data by converting it into an unreadable format. This data can only be deciphered by those who possess the corresponding encryption key. This method is integral to the operation of a blockchain, as it ensures that data within the blockchain remains confidential and that unauthorized users cannot edit or forge information within the blockchain.

Cryptography involves two key types: Symmetric key cryptography and asymmetric key cryptography.

Symmetric key cryptography is when the same key is used for both encryption and decryption. Meanwhile, asymmetric key cryptography, also known as public key cryptography, involves a pair of keys - a public key that everyone can access and a private key that remains confidential.

4.2. The Importance of Hash Functions

A fundamental aspect of cryptographic security is the hash function. A hash function is a unique type of function that takes an input and produces an output of a fixed length, regardless of the size of the input, ensuring all data is protected equally.

Crucially, these hash functions work only in one direction. This means that, with the output alone, even the most powerful supercomputers lack the ability to work in reverse and derive the original input from a hash function's output.

Blockchains leverage this feature extensively. For example, each block in a blockchain contains a number of transactions, each with its unique hash. The integrity of these blocks is thereby maintained, as altering even a single bit of data changes the corresponding hash completely.

4.3. Cryptography in Blockchain: Digital Signatures

A key application of cryptography in blockchain is the digital signature. Upon creating a new transaction to be added to the blockchain, the sender will provide a digital signature alongside the data itself. This digital signature serves as a type of secure seal, providing evidence that the transaction was indeed initiated by the sender.

To produce a digital signature, a sender will first create a hash of the data to be sent. They will then encrypt this hash with their private key, resulting in the digital signature. Upon receiving this, the recipient can use the sender's public key to decrypt the digital signature, revealing the original hash.

Marvellously, if the decrypted hash matches the hash of the received data when it too is hashed, the recipient can be certain that the data was not tampered with during transit.

4.4. Cryptography in Blockchain: Consensus Mechanisms

Cryptography also provides the foundation for the consensus mechanisms that govern how new blocks are added to the blockchain. One of the most well-known consensus mechanisms is the Proof-of-Work method, utilised by Bitcoin.

In Proof-of-Work, miners must solve computationally intensive puzzles to gain the right to add new blocks to the blockchain. These puzzles are hash functions, with the challenge being to find a hash below a certain target value. To do so, miners must vary their input until they stumble upon a valid output, a process that requires substantial computational resources.

4.5. Keys to Your Crypto Kingdom: Wallets and Private Keys

Your private key is akin to the most secure password you can imagine. This key is employed to sign transactions and thereby provides definitive proof that they truly originated from you. However, the caveat here is, if someone else gains access to your private key, they can effectively pretend to be you and steal all your digital assets.

Therefore, how you manage your private keys is crucial to the security of your digital assets in the crypto world. These keys are often stored in digital wallets, with many wallet solutions offering extra layers of security, such as password protection or biometric identification, to guard your private keys.

However, the critical principle is this: It is your responsibility to safeguard your private keys, for losing them means losing access to your digital assets forever.

4.6. Take-Away: Cryptography is the Bedrock of Blockchain Security

To wrap up, cryptography is undoubtedly the cornerstone of blockchain security. It is the driving force behind the confidentiality, integrity, and authenticity of data in the blockchain. By leveraging an intricate network of hash functions, digital signatures, and consensus mechanisms, blockchain technology can offer an unprecedented level of security and trust within the digital realm.

However, the security offered by cryptography is not infallible. Users must remain vigilant and establish robust security practices to protect their private keys and digital assets adequately. Remember, ignorance is an exploitable vulnerability in the crypto world, so understanding cryptographic security is vital to your journey in the blockchain voyage.

Chapter 5. Evaluating the Security Spectrum of Blockchain Applications

In the dynamic world of blockchain and crypto technology, understanding the security spectrum is integral. We begin by considering the reality that no system is impervious to breaches or attacks; each possesses its own susceptibilities. Therefore, the question isn't whether the system is vulnerable, but rather how we minimize the risks and maximize security potential.

5.1. Understanding Blockchain Security

The inherent security measures in the blockchain infrastructure stem from its foundational aspects, such as decentralized control, cryptographic protocols, and consensus algorithms. While these aspects provide layers of security, understanding their scope and limitations is critical in evaluating the overall security of any blockchain application.

Decentralization mitigates single point of failure risks as data isn't located in one central server. However, it also opens the door to potential network-wide attacks, such as the 51% attack, where an entity gaining control of over half of the network nodes can manipulate the blockchain.

Cryptographic protocols, while robust, rely on the strength of the algorithm and the secrecy of the keys. Thus, blockchain applications are highly susceptible to attacks that attempt to break these cryptographic conventions – such as quantum computing-based attacks or brute force attacks.

Consensus algorithms like Proof of Work or Proof of Stake ensure that all participants agree on the validity of transactions. However, they are not without their weak points. Issues such as the 'Nothing-At-Stake' problem and 'Long-Range Attacks' present potential attack vectors for those with enough resources and motivation to target a blockchain.

5.2. Vulnerabilities in Smart Contracts

Smart contracts, codes that automatically execute upon meeting predefined conditions, are another aspect of blockchain ecosystems that requires scrutiny. Though designed to remove intermediaries and reduce fraud, they introduce new vulnerabilities due to coding errors, incomplete function definitions, and open-ends that can be misused.

Poorly-written or inadequately-audited smart contracts have proven disastrous in the past, exemplifying the notorious DAO Attack, where an attacker exploited a smart contract bug to drain millions of dollars worth of Ether.

5.3. Safeguarding Wallets and Exchanges

Security lapses aren't limited to the blockchain network itself. Wallets—both software and hardware—are subject to attack. It ranges from digital attacks like phishing and malware to physical threats like theft or loss. Wallets, although necessary for interacting with blockchain, need proper security protocols: strong passwords, multi-factor authentication, and regular backups.

Exchanges, where cryptocurrencies change hands, are also vulnerable. Centralized exchanges, in particular, are attractive targets for hackers due to the mass amount of cryptocurrencies they handle. Decentralized exchanges present a different kind of risk, as their anonymity can be abused for nefarious activities, such as money laundering.

5.4. Evolving Threats & Security Responses

Cryptocurrency mining malware, advanced ransomware schemes, and phishing attacks exemplify the unconventional and constantly evolving threats facing the crypto realm. It necessitates an equivalent evolution in security responses, like the employment of advanced malware detection tools, the integration of AI in security protocols, and continuous education on phishing and scam trends.

One promising but largely unexplored solution is leveraging quantum computing for securing blockchains. Given its potential to break traditional cryptographic security, it holds promise to reinforce security against the same threat when used defensively.

5.5. Regulation and Security

The role of regulation in securing blockchain ecosystems is paramount. Without a uniform regulatory approach, the global and decentralized nature of blockchain facilitates illicit activities and makes prosecution difficult. Moreover, lack of regulation leaves users of blockchain applications unprotected from scams, fraud, and market manipulation.

Regulatory bodies around the world are making strides in introducing cryptocurrency and blockchain-specific regulations. However, it's a delicate balancing act between ensuring security and stifling innovation. The appropriate regulation encourages robust security practices, provides user protection, and fosters an environment conducive to innovation and growth.

Reflecting on the security spectrum of blockchain applications, it's clear that the landscape is multifaceted, continually evolving, and fraught with potential risks. However, with meticulous assessment and proactive measures, these risks can be minimized and the immense potential of blockchain technology can be realized safely. We encourage every participant, whether a potential investor, developer, or casual user, to stay vigilant and informed. Awareness is, after all, one of the fundamental pillars of security.

Chapter 6. Attacks on Blockchain: Case Studies of Notorious Breaches

The complexity and depth of blockchain technology make it a strong and secure method of transmitting information. However, like all digital constructs, it is not entirely impervious to attacks. As we delve into this chapter, we'll dissect infamous instances where blockchain security was compromised, enabling us a precious opportunity to learn from these retaliations and further bolster the walls of blockchain applications.

6.1. The DAO Attack

Let's start with one of the most infamous tales in the world of blockchain, the case of The Decentralized Autonomous Organization (DAO), which serves as a reminder of how software loopholes can lead to massive losses.

The DAO was a decentralized venture capital fund, built on the Ethereum blockchain, designed to leverage smart contracts to eliminate the need for traditional governance and management. In April 2016, DAO announced an Initial Coin Offering (ICO) and accumulated nearly $150 million in Ethereum. However, by June, an unknown entity exploited a vulnerability known as the 'Recursive Call Exploit.'

The vulnerability allowed the attacker to drain more than 3.6 million Ether (around $50 million at that time) from The DAO into a subsidiary account known as a 'Child DAO.' Surprisingly, the code exploited was not a bug but rather an overlooked feature of the smart contract that let it interact recursively with itself. While the Ethereum community eventually neutralized the attack, the incident left a significant scar on the industry and underlined the need for stringent code reviewing measures in blockchain applications.

6.2. The Mt. Gox Breach

Mt. Gox was once the world's largest Bitcoin exchange, handling over 70% of all Bitcoin transactions worldwide. However, its name is now synonymous with one of the most significant security breaches in crypto history.

Between 2011 and 2014, the exchange was a victim of ongoing hacking attacks that remained unnoticed for several years. The hackers stole approximately 740,000 Bitcoins (around $460 million at the time and $28 billion as of November 2021) via a transaction malleability attack, exploiting a known but unaddressed flaw in the Bitcoin protocol itself.

Though the issue with transaction malleability was known beforehand, the Mt.Gox team failed to implement measures to counter it adequately, leading to their downfall. This breach, coupled with ineffective crisis management, resulted in Mt.Gox filing for bankruptcy in 2014, causing a massive blow to the trust in Bitcoin and cryptocurrencies more broadly.

6.3. The Bitfinex Hack

Up next is the infamous Bitfinex hack of 2016, wherein losses amounted to nearly 120,000 Bitcoins (around $72 million back then). The attack was orchestrated through an exploitation on Bitfinex's system, which used a multi-signature system for withdrawals.

In this case, the hackers creatively bypassed security by gaining access to two of the three keys required for transactions— one from Bitfinex and one from Bitgo, the company responsible for the application's security. Following the attack, Bitcoin's value dropped by 20%, offering us a vivid example of how such breaches can significantly impact the wider crypto market.

6.4. The Coincheck Heist

In January 2018, the Japanese crypto exchange Coincheck reported losses of 523 million NEM coins (approximately $534 million at that time), marking the biggest hack in history, dwarfing even that of Mt.Gox.

Coincheck largely attributed the loss to weak security practices, particularly their decision to store the assets in a hot wallet (online) rather than in more secure cold storage. Additionally, the exchange did not use multi-sig wallets or smart contracts. Later investigations found that the hackers had managed to infect the employees' personal computers with a virus, leading to the theft.

The Coincheck breach emphasizes the importance of adopting recommended security measures like cold storage and multi-sig wallets – a vital point for any blockchain practitioner looking to safely hold or transact vast crypto assets.

6.5. The Parity Wallet Vulnerability

Lastly, we look at the Parity wallet incident, often referred to as the $280 million bug. In November 2017, a user exploited a hole in Parity's Ethereum wallet library contract and converted the WalletLibrary contract into a multi-sig wallet. This user then claimed ownership and deleted the code, consequently rendering all multi-sig contracts unusable and freezing around 513,774 Ether.

The incident underscores the potential risks of complex smart contracts and also the importance of thorough auditing and testing of these contracts in the real world.

In conclusion, while blockchain applications promise high levels of security, these instances underline the fact that they are not foolproof. These case studies serve as teachable events for blockchain developers, who are urged to recognize the potential for exploitation in their systems and work accordingly to harden their implementations.

Chapter 7. Exploring the Future of Crypto Security: Quantum Computing

As we steer our conversation in the direction of the future, one crucial and looming technological advancement stands out: quantum computing. Undeniably, its potential paves the way for a redefined horizon in encryption and security systems, throwing open new considerations and challenges for cryptocurrencies and blockchain technologies.

7.1. The Quantum Future and Cryptocurrencies

Quantum computers fundamentally differ from contemporary computers. They leverage the superposition principle in quantum mechanics to process exponentially more information than traditional computers. The encryption systems that secure our current internet, including cryptocurrencies, are based on complex mathematical problems that are easy for a computer to solve in one direction but considered impossible to break the other way.

However, steps are being made to ensure the compatibility of this promising future technology with our current cryptographic systems. Quantum-resistant cryptographic algorithms, also known as post-quantum cryptography, is a fast-emerging field aiming to construct algorithms that can withstand the computational prowess of quantum computers.

7.2. Quantifying Quantum Threats

Let's first recognize the nature and magnitude of the threat that quantum computing poses. The quintessential cryptographic algorithms used in blockchain tech, such as the Elliptic Curve Digital Signature Algorithm (ECDSA), are theoretically at risk from the brute force attack power of quantum machines. The principal risk hinges on the capacity of quantum computers to solve the so-called 'factoring problem' exponentially faster than existing technologies.

For cryptocurrencies, two primary vulnerabilities exist. The first concerns private key derivation from public keys; if a transaction awaiting inclusion in a block reveals the public key, a well-resourced quantum attacker could derive the corresponding private key and change the transaction details. Second, mined blocks that yet have to be added to a blockchain likewise reveal public keys and are susceptible to similar attacks.

7.3. Preparing for the Quantum Leap

Notwithstanding the potential threats, several encouraging initiatives prepare us for a quantum future. Deploying quantum-resistant algorithms on a large scale remains a work in progress, and more research is needed to achieve optimal safety standards.

Strategies like address re-use prevention can offer simple yet effective safeguards. Bitcoin already implements this; after a transaction takes place, remaining funds are transferred to a new address, eliminating the risk of quantum attacks since quantum machines could, in theory, only target a public key associated with spent funds.

Code-based, multivariate quadratic, hash-based, lattice-based, and secret-key cryptography schemes are all promising quantum-resistant solutions. They are under active consideration for building quantum-resistant blockchain systems.

7.4. Realistic Timelines and Interim Measures

Although a fully functional, universal quantum computer remains a distant reality, it is obvious that we need to start building quantum-resistant cryptography now. In the meantime, hybrid systems combining traditional and quantum-resistant cryptography could be a viable solution. This ensures ongoing security and will smoothen the transition when the time comes.

7.5. Quantum Computing and Blockchain: A Symbiotic Relationship

Quantum computing does not just spell disaster for cryptography. The technology could be applied to optimize mining processes by searching for nonces swiftly. Its potential usage extends to running complex smart contracts or aiding layer-two solutions on blockchains.

Quite remarkably, blockchain technology could enhance quantum computing — or more precisely, secure quantum networks. Quantum key distribution (QKD) could make use of blockchain's immutable feature to preserve data integrity, positioning blockchain as a feasible solution for securing QKD.

In conclusion, the intersection of the quantum computing and blockchain spaces poses unique challenges and extraordinary opportunities. Thorough research, careful planning, and foresight are vital to unlock these prospects and to safeguard against potential vulnerabilities for a secure, thriving future in a world where quantum computing and cryptography coexist. The journey promises to be intriguing, if not surprising. Endurance and a continual quest for learning will be our best aids as we move forward into this uncharted territory.

Remember, while the quantum threat is real and frightening, it is not an immediate concern, and it certainly is not insurmountable. The crypto landscape is already beginning to evolve and adapt, signifying the beginning of an exciting chapter that we call the "Quantum Future".

Chapter 8. The Regulatory Landscape of Cryptocurrencies and Blockchain

The regulatory environment surrounding cryptocurrencies and blockchain technology is as diverse and complex as the technology itself. As this digital revolution continues to galvanize industries worldwide, regulators are grappling to establish structures that strike the right balance between fostering innovation and preventing illicit activities.

8.1. Cryptocurrencies: Perception and Classification

One reason for the often muddled regulatory landscape is the varied perception and classification of cryptocurrencies. Some jurisdictions view cryptocurrencies as commodities, some as securities, while others classify them as currencies. This inconsistency stems from the myriad uses for cryptocurrencies - as a store of value (much like gold or other commodities), a medium for conducting transactions (akin to traditional currencies), or as tokens used in Initial Coin Offerings (ICOs) that provide utility within a specific ecosystem or represent stake in a company (like securities).

In the United States, most cryptocurrencies are treated as property for tax purposes by the Internal Revenue Service (IRS), while the Commodity Futures Trading Commission (CFTC) considers Bitcoin a commodity. On the other hand, the Securities and Exchange Commission (SEC) has indicated that it deems many ICOs to be securities offerings subject to its regulations.

Across the pond in the European Union, there's no uniform classification of cryptocurrencies. In Germany, Bitcoin has legal recognition as a 'unit of account', making it taxable regardless of whether it's used as a medium of exchange. In the UK, cryptocurrencies are considered foreign currency for tax purposes if used as a payment method.

8.2. Blockchain Applications: Regulatory Implications

Regulatory implications for blockchain applications extend beyond cryptocurrencies. Blockchain technology's potential to disrupt multiple industries presents unique regulatory conundrums.

For instance, distributed ledger technology (DLT), which includes blockchain, is used in supply chain management to track goods at every stage of production and shipment. These applications, however, may encounter data protection regulations like Europe's General Data Protection Regulation (GDPR), which enforces the 'right to erasure', a concept potentially incompatible with DLT's immutable records.

Likewise, in the financial sector, Decentralised Finance (DeFi) - blockchain-based, algorithmically driven financial platforms without intermediaries - is on the rise. Regulators are still formulating strategies to manage DeFi platforms which operate on smart contracts, automatically executing transactions when pre-set conditions are met. This brings into focus questions of accountability and conflict resolution without centralized authorities.

8.3. Global Regulatory Approaches

Regulatory approaches towards cryptocurrencies and blockchain technology vary worldwide, reflecting each jurisdiction's attitude towards this disruptive innovation.

Some countries, like Malta and Switzerland, have embraced cryptocurrencies and blockchain technology, hoping to become global frontrunners in this emerging industry. They've adopted friendly regulations and created fast-tracked licensing procedures, attracting numerous crypto-startups.

Others like China and India have taken a more territorial approach. China, despite being home to a majority of the global Bitcoin mining operations, has imposed a blanket ban on cryptocurrencies. India had initially banned banks from dealing with cryptocurrency businesses, but the Supreme Court overturned the restriction in 2020. However, regulatory uncertainties remain.

In contrast, countries like the U.S and Japan are aiming for a measured approach. While Japan has established a crypto-friendly legal environment, it has stringent licensing procedures and trading practices. The U.S, still working on its comprehensive regulatory framework, has often contradicted stances among its regulatory bodies, but efforts for clearer regulations are underway.

8.4. Challenges and Future Directions

The diverse and complex regulatory landscape of cryptocurrencies and blockchain technology brings forth several challenges. The decentralization and cross-border nature of these technologies pose difficulties in establishing jurisdiction, enforcement, and punishing non-compliance.

This calls for international regulatory cooperation that can tap the benefits of these technologies while mitigating risks. Inter-governmental organizations like the Financial Action Task Force (FATF) have already begun creating guidelines for global standards on regulating virtual assets and providers.

As we delve deeper into the digital era, it's crucial that regulators take a flexible, adaptable approach. Initially, a principle-based rather than rule-based approach may be more suitable, thereby providing broad standards to guide the industry and leaving space for innovation.

The crypto arms race is quickly evolving, with security standards and regulatory norms trying to keep pace. Navigating this landscape isn't simple, but with the right knowledge, this domain's potential is immense and unignorable. As the ecosystem continues to flourish, regulatory dynamics will inexorably shape the sector's future, paving the way for broader technological transformation.

Thus, as cryptocurrencies and blockchain technology continue to gain momentum, the pressing need for a sound regulatory framework has never been more apparent. This delicate balancing act between governance and growth, regulatory control and financial freedom, forms a critical juncture in the path of digital evolution.

Chapter 9. Securing Personal Crypto Assets: Practical Tips

The safeguarding of your personal crypto assets is a task not to be taken lightly. Often, people may not pay enough attention to this because they think that blockchain is 'unhackable.' However, despite the robust structure of the blockchain, it is not completely immune to attacks. Ensuring that your crypto investments are secure is essential to avoid potential losses. Let's delve into the practicalities about how to better secure your crypto assets.

9.1. Securing Your Wallets

The first step to securing your crypto assets is to protect your digital wallet. There are several types of wallets available, and it's essential to know about them to make conscious choices. One popular option is hardware wallets, which store your private key offline. It's among the most secure options since it significantly reduces the chances of being hacked.

Another common choice is software wallets, which are programs that you can install on your mobile device or computer. Although not as secure as hardware wallets due to the online connection, they can still provide an optimal level of security if used with caution. However, they increase the need for excellent antivirus software and a very paranoid approach to email attachments and websites.

Whatever wallet type you choose, ensure that its encryption is in line with the latest security standards. Regularly updating your wallet software can also ensure that it includes all the recently released security enhancements.

9.2. Understand Private Keys

Private keys play a prominent role in the security of your crypto assets. They are what you use to sign off on transactions, and losing them could mean losing access to your crypto permanently.

It's vital to keep your private keys secret. Never share them with anyone, and avoid storing them online where they could be vulnerable to theft. Instead, consider writing them down and storing them in a physically secure place.

Remember, your wallet doesn't actually store your cryptocurrency. It only holds the private key that gives you access to the transactions linked to your cryptocurrency on the blockchain. As such, losing this key means you lose your cryptocurrency.

9.3. Secure Internet Connection

When dealing with crypto, ensure that your connection to the internet is secure at all times. It's best to avoid using public Wi-Fi for cryptocurrency transactions, as these networks are often unsecure and may expose your data to potential hackers.

If you have to use such networks, consider using a virtual private network (VPN). A VPN can encrypt your data and safeguard it from prying eyes. Remember that even seemingly secure Wi-Fi networks can have vulnerabilities, so always err on the side of caution.

9.4. Two-Factor Authentication

Two-Factor Authentication (2FA) is a crucial step in protecting your crypto assets. It adds an extra layer to your security, requiring more than just a username and password.

Often, this second layer is a code sent to your mobile device, making it much harder for potential hackers to gain access to your data. Many crypto exchange platforms and wallets offer 2FA, and it's usually just a matter of enabling it in your security settings.

9.5. Regularly Monitor Crypto Activities

Keeping a close eye on your digital assets will help you identify any irregularities which could indicate a security breach. Use the blockchain's public ledger to track your transactions, and make sure to verify all incoming and outgoing operations.

Additionally, monitor news feeds and subscribe to relevant updates to stay aware of the latest crypto-related scams and potential vulnerabilities in the market.

9.6. Do Not Share Information Publicly

Finally, it is always good to remember that in the digital age, oversharing personal info can lead to trouble. Avoid talking about your investments in public forums or on social media where potential attackers may be lurking.

It's also a good idea to use distinct addresses for different transactions. This way, you can avoid linking your entire balance to a single address, which could be revealed to the public.

Securing your crypto assets might seem daunting at first, but with these tips in mind, you'll be ready to take necessary actions to ensure your crypto assets are well guarded. Remember, in the ever-evolving world of cryptocurrency, vigilance and a proactive approach to security are your best defenses.

Chapter 10. Institutional Approaches to Crypto Application Security

As the overall financial landscape continues to shape itself around digital assets, an increasing number of institutions are picking up pace to secure their investments and infrastructural capabilities. The institutional approaches to crypto application security fall into two main focus areas: preventive security techniques and correctives actions after security breaches.

10.1. Preventive Security Techniques for Institutional Crypto Applications

Preventive security techniques focus on taking various actions to prevent security issues from happening before they occur.

1. Technical Measures

One dominant method employed by institutions today is encryption. Encryption algorithms ensure that only authorized participants can read and write transactions to the network. Examples include the SHA-256 protocol used by Bitcoin and the Scrypt protocol in Litecoin. Institutions also invest heavily in secure hardware to protect their digital assets. These include multi-signature wallets that require signatures from multiple parties to sign a transaction.

1. Regulatory Measures

From a regulatory perspective, institutions follow a stringent KYC (Know Your Customer) protocol and employ AML (Anti-Money

Laundering) practices. These measures help to prevent fraudulent activities by validating identities and tracking unusual money flows. Due diligence is essential to verify that crypto applications and coins conform with international laws and regulations.

1. Internal Controls

Institutions implement strict internal controls to ensure security at an organizational layer. These include access controls that limit who can access specific information, segregation of duties to prevent a single person from controlling all parts of a financial transaction, and risk management controls.

10.2. Corrective Actions post-security breaches

Despite best efforts, intrusions can happen. Corrective actions post-security breaches are crucial to limit the damage done and re-establish security protocols.

1. Incident Response

Incident response is the process of identifying, investigating, and responding to cyber threats. It involves quickly and accurately diagnosing the cause of an incident, neutralizing threats, and restoring normal operations.

1. Legal Actions

These involve pursuing legal recourse against attackers. Legal actions not only help the institution recover their lost assets but serve to deter potential malicious actors. Furthermore, firms often engage in continual legal monitoring to ensure the most updated laws regulate their crypto activities.

1. Audit and Assurance

Institutions regularly conduct audits to understand their weaknesses and develop robust strategies to mitigate them. These include internal audits, third-party audits, and blockchain-specific audits that scrutinize the security of smart contracts. Crypto-specific certifications also add to the overall assurance of an institution's security level.

10.3. Adoption of Advanced Technologies

From the perspective of bolstering security, institutions further explore advanced technology solutions.

1. Quantum Computing

Quantum computing, capable of processing vast amounts of data simultaneously, poses both a threat and opportunity. While its computational prowess could potentially break traditional cryptographic defenses in the future, quantum techniques also hold the potential to build unconditionally secure cryptography.

1. AI and ML

Artificial Intelligence (AI) and Machine Learning (ML) are being used in risk detection, predicting malicious activities, and enhancing security practices. They can be trained to identify patterns of cyberattacks and take preemptive measures before the threat penetrates the network.

1. Blockchain-based Security

Blockchain technology itself provides inherent security benefits due to its decentralized nature and transparency. Institutional investors explore the use of blockchain to enhance their security protocols, such as transaction tracking, automated regulatory compliance, and secure data storage.

Crypto application security goes beyond just the technical measures. Although constant vigilance and real-time corrective actions are necessary, preventive measures form the bedrock of security. The precise recipe for crypto security consists of a mix of proactive measures, technological advancements, as well as robust post-incident actions. Institutions must foster a culture of security that permeates an understanding of the volatile crypto sphere and the uniqueness of each blockchain application they venture into. By doing so, they can stay ahead in the crypto arms race and ensure safe navigation in the exciting realm of digital assets.

Chapter 11. The Road Ahead: Predictions and Preparations

As blockchain technology and cryptocurrencies evolve at an unprecedented pace, it's time we ponder on what lies ahead. Let's dive into some projections for this fast-paced industry and discuss how you can prepare.

11.1. The Ongoing Battle of Quantum Computing

Blockchain's reliability is partly due to the computational difficulty involved in tampering with encrypted data blocks containing millions of bits of information. However, this security principle could be challenged by the advent of quantum computing. Boasting computing power significantly surpassing today's machines, quantum computers could crack complex calculations and encryption techniques that currently ensure blockchain's security. Yet the race is not lost. Blockchain developers are adopting quantum-resistant cryptographic methods, safeguarding the technology from potential quantum threats.

11.2. Interoperability and Cross-Chain Technology

Traditionally, blockchains like Bitcoin and Ethereum operate independently, leading to fragmentation issues. Interoperability is one solution, allowing data to seamlessly move across different blockchain networks, thereby optimizing efficiency, scalability, and cost. Protocols like Cosmos and Polkadot are already enabling cross-chain transactions, heralding a new era of interconnectedness and synergy. As such, participating in multiple blockchains or diversifying your crypto portfolio may prove beneficial.

11.3. Increased Regulation and Legal Recognition

As cryptocurrencies mature, regulatory bodies worldwide are exerting tighter control, aiming to integrate digital currencies into the conventional financial fabric. This transformation may result in dynamic legal landscapes, tax liabilities, and added consumer protections. Cryptocurrency users and investors should be prepared to navigate these evolving norms and guidelines, making detailed knowledge of local and international regulations critical.

11.4. Rise of Decentralized Finance (DeFi)

DeFi, a blockchain trend, is set to shape the digital financial ecosystem, eliminating intermediaries and offering financial services to those otherwise excluded. From novel savings products to tokenized assets, DeFi unlocks innovative investment possibilities. However, the nascent sector is fraught with risks, including high volatility and complex smart contracts. As DeFi becomes mainstream, users must polish their understanding while adopting prudent risk management strategies.

11.5. Advanced Security Measures and Best Practices

As cyber threats increase, blockchain applications developers will lean heavily on advanced security measures, including multi-signature wallets, hardware wallets, and two-factor authentications. Security measures and best practices will continue to be a vital topic of discussion for all stakeholders. Users must continually update themselves and prioritize secure platforms while being aware of the latest in cybersecurity.

11.6. Mainstream Adoption of Blockchain

Driven by countless real-world applications, from supply chain tracking to voting systems, blockchain stands on the brink of mainstream adoption. Businesses may need to strategically align their operations with this technology to stay competitive. Similarly, individual participants need to gear up for an increased use of blockchain-based services.

11.7. Impact of Environmental Concerns

Cryptocurrencies, particularly Bitcoin, have drawn criticism for their high energy consumption. The world is shifting towards a greener economy, and so is the crypto world. Ethereum, the second-biggest cryptocurrency, is leading this transformation with its plan to switch to Proof of Stake (PoS) mechanism that would use less energy. Green crypto, or crypto-assets pegged to environmental, social, and governance (ESG) initiatives, are gaining momentum. Decisions on entering the crypto market should thus factor in these sustainability concerns.

11.8. Evolution of Central Bank Digital Currencies (CBDCs)

With the rise of digital currencies, central banks are exploring CBDCs that combine cryptocurrency's efficiency with state-backed guarantee of value. Proliferation of CBDCs could directly affect the dynamics of conventional cryptocurrencies. Encouragingly, CBDCs could lead to increased recognition and adoption of crypto. Embracing these inevitable shifts could be vital to future-proofing one's participation in the digital assets ecosystem.

Throughout this winding journey, success in the world of blockchain and crypto will be greatly dependent on adaptability, knowledge, and diligence. As this chapter reveals, the landscape is set to be complex, exciting, and innately promising. Regardless of the variety of prospective paths and the number of questions that remain, one thing is clear: Blockchain and cryptocurrencies will continue to transform our world in unpredictable yet remarkable ways.